cloverleaf books™

Community Helpers

Let's Meet a Doctor

Bridget Heos

illustrated by Mike Moran

M MILLBROOK PRESS · MINNEAPOLIS

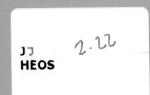
With thanks to Dr. Stephen Lauer
and Jill Chadwick —B.H.

Millbrook Press
A division of Lerner Publishing Group, Inc.
241 First Avenue North
Minneapolis, MN 55401 U.S.A.

Website address: www.lernerbooks.com

Main body text set in Slappy Inline 18/28.
Typeface provided by T26.

Library of Congress Cataloging-in-Publication Data

Heos, Bridget.
    Let's meet a doctor / by Bridget Heos ; illustrated by Mike
Moran.
        p.   cm. — (Cloverleaf books—community helpers)
    Includes index.
    ISBN 978–0–7613–9028–2 (lib. bdg. : alk. paper)
    1. Pediatricians—Juvenile literature. 2. Physicians—Juvenile
literature. I. Moran, Michael, 1957– ill. II. Title.
RJ78.H46 2013
618.92—dc23   2012019099

Manufactured in the United States of America
1 – BP – 12/31/12

TABLE OF CONTENTS

Chapter One

The Youngest Patients

Our class is on a mission. We want to find out what a **doctor** does.

We decide to talk to Dr. Zambil. He's a pediatrician. That's a doctor who treats children.

Doctors are workers in the community. A community is a group of people who live in the same city, town, or neighborhood.

"I help kids feel their best," he says.

"How do you do that?" asks Jayden.

Dr. Zambil explains by telling us about his day.

Dr. Zambil works in a **clinic**. He sees about twenty **patients** each day.

They are babies, children, and teenagers. Some are **sick** or **hurt**.

"I find out what's wrong," he says. "They may need **medicine.** They may need to rest. Sometimes they need to go to the **hospital.**"

Doctors write prescriptions for medicine. A prescription tells a pharmacist what medicine a patient needs. It also tells the patient when to take the medicine.

J.J. raises his hand. "I went to the **hospital** when I was little. But I'm better now."

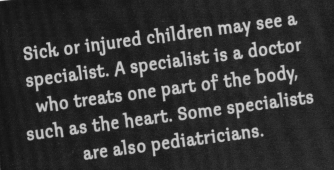

Sick or injured children may see a specialist. A specialist is a doctor who treats one part of the body, such as the heart. Some specialists are also pediatricians.

"Good!" Dr. Zambil says. "That's our goal. We want you to be **healthy** so you can reach your goals too."

"My goal is to be a tightrope walker!" Nick says.

"Uh-oh!" Dr. Zambil says.

Chapter Two
Checkups

"I went to the doctor when I wasn't sick," Katya says.

"That's good," Dr. Zambil says. "Kids should see a doctor once a year for **checkups**."

HEALTHY FOOD

He checks their ears. He listens to their hearts. He asks if they eat healthy food. He asks if they run around. These things help kids stay well.

Doctors examine ears with a tool called an otoscope. They listen to the heart with a stethoscope.

"Do you give kids **shots?**" Paul asks.

Shots make you immune to some diseases, such as measles. That means your body protects itself from the germs that cause the disease.

"Nurses do," Dr. Zambil says. "They took classes.
They know how to make the **shots hurt less.**"

Chapter Three

Doctor School

"Did you have to take classes too?" asks Paul.

"Yes, lots of them!" Dr. Zambil says.

We learn that Dr. Zambil went to grade school for nine years, high school for four years, and college for four years.

Medical school lasts four years. Then students become residents and fellows. They see patients. Other doctors help them. This takes three to ten years.

Then he had medical school and training for seven years.

That's twenty-four years of school. And a lot of homework!

"When I'm not at the clinic, I teach," Dr. Zambil says.
"Like Ms. Nguyen," we say, looking at our teacher.
"Yes, but I don't teach in a classroom," he says.

"I teach at the hospital. My students learn to be doctors by seeing real patients."

Medical students spend time at a hospital during every year of medical school. Experienced doctors teach them how to treat patients.

17

Lainey raises her hand. "I was a real patient. I went to the hospital when **I broke my arm.**"

"You probably had an **X-ray**." Dr. Zambil holds one up.

X-rays are pictures that show the bones and organs inside your body. But most of the time, these aren't needed during a visit to the doctor.

We all want to tell Dr. Zambil about our injuries. But he has to go see patients. And we have to go to recess. Running around keeps us **healthy!**

Because Dr. Zambil lends a hand to help us feel our best, we give him a hand.

Make Your Own Stethoscope

Doctors use a stethoscope to listen to a patient's heart, lungs, and stomach. This helps them make sure the body is healthy. You can make a stethoscope at home. Use it to listen to your own heart beating!

What you need:
2 small funnels with ⅜-inch (1 centimeter) spouts
scissors
1 balloon
duct tape or electrical tape
2 feet (0.6 meters) of ½-inch (1 ¼ cm) plastic flexible tubing

1) Have an adult snip off the narrow tip of the balloon with scissors. Then stretch the balloon top over the wide opening of one funnel. The balloon should be flat and tight. Use tape to hold the balloon in place.

2) Fit one funnel into each end of the tubing. Tape the funnels to the tubing to hold them in place.

3) Now, test your stethoscope. Put the balloon funnel over your heart. (Your heart is just to the left of the center of your chest.) Put the open funnel over your ear. Can you hear your heart?

4) Run around for a few minutes, and then listen to your heart again. Can you hear it beating faster? Try listening to your mom or dad's heart too.

GLOSSARY

diseases: sicknesses with specific causes and symptoms

doctor: a person who diagnoses and treats health problems in people

fellows: doctors who learn a specialty from more experienced doctors

immune: protected against a disease

medicine: substances swallowed or put on the skin to treat an illness or injury

nurse: a person who is trained to care for the sick or injured and to help others stay healthy

otoscope: a handheld tool with a light inside a tube. Doctors use it to examine the ear.

patients: people who receive medical care

pediatrician: a doctor who specializes in the care of children

pharmacist: a person who prepares medicine

prescriptions: instructions for preparing and taking medicine

residents: doctors in their first few years after finishing medical school. They treat patients and learn from more experienced doctors.

specialist: a doctor who treats a specific part of the body, such as the heart

stethoscope: a tool that a doctor uses to listen to the heart, lungs, and other organs

X-ray: a picture that shows teeth, bones, and organs inside the body

BOOKS

Bellisario, Gina. *Let's Meet a Veterinarian.* Minneapolis: Millbrook Press, 2013.
Find out what work is like for a veterinarian, a doctor who treats animals.

Goldish, Meish. *Doctors to the Rescue.* New York: Bearport, 2011.
Learn about doctors who respond to emergencies.

Salzmann, Mary Elizabeth. *Doctor's Tools.* Minneapolis: Abdo Publishing Company, 2011.
Explore how otoscopes, stethoscopes, thermometers, and other tools help doctors do their job.

WEBSITES

BAM! Body and Mind
http://www.bam.gov/index.html
Learn about health, safety, exercise, and disease through features and activities on this site from the Centers for Disease Control and Prevention.

Going to the Doctor
http://kidshealth.org/kid/feel_better/people/going_to_dr.html#
Find out what to expect during a visit to the doctor, and learn what different parts of a checkup tell the doctor about your health.

Kidnetic.com
http://kidnetic.com/
Get moving with games created by kids, and find fun, tasty things to eat that will keep you healthy!

LERNER SOURCE

Expand learning beyond the printed book. Download free, complementary educational resources for this book from our website, www.lernersource.com.